A Look
Round the Estate

A Look
Round the Estate

Poems 1957-1967

KINGSLEY AMIS

HARCOURT, BRACE & WORLD, INC.
NEW YORK

To Jane
and Karl Miller

ACKNOWLEDGMENTS

are made to the editors respectively of the *Spectator*, the *New Statesman*, *Encounter*, the *London Magazine* and *Listen*, in one or other of which most of these poems were first printed. Some of the poems in 'The Evans Country' appeared in a pamphlet of that title, published by the Fantasy Press, Oxford, in 1962.

CONTENTS

A Look
Round the Estate

An Ever-Fixed Mark

Years ago, at a private school
Run on traditional lines,
One fellow used to perform
Prodigious feats in the dorm;
His quite undevious designs
Found many a willing tool.

On the rugger field, in the gym,
Buck marked down at his leisure
The likeliest bits of stuff;
The notion, familiar enough,
Of 'using somebody for pleasure'
Seemed handy and harmless to him.

But another chap was above
The diversions of such a lout;
Seven years in the place
And he never got to first base
With the kid he followed about:
What interested Ralph was love.

He did the whole thing in style –
Letters three times a week,
Sonnet-sequences, Sunday walks;
Then, during one of their talks,
The youngster caressed his cheek,
And that made it all worth while.

These days, for a quid pro quo,
Ralph's chum is all for romance;
Buck's playmates, family men,
Eye a Boy Scout now and then.
Sex stops when you pull up your pants,
Love never lets you go.

Out-Patient

Can you stand sanity, committee virtue,
Married, seeing its way, good-humoured
And humouring, over forty
Thank God, enough to drive you mad,

Or insanity with its Look at me
While I do my thing to you or I give up?
Right then, mine's a lobotomy.

Please, there are no midways;
Visit either, like the other.

Change is for kids.

A Tribute to the Founder

By bluster, graft, and doing people down,
Sam Baines got rich, but, mellowing at last,
Felt that by giving something to the town
He might undo the evils of his past.

His hope was to prevent the local youth
From making the mistakes that he had made:
Choosing expediency instead of truth,
And quitting what was honest for what paid.

A university seemed just the thing,
And that old stately home the very place.
Sam wept with pleasure at its opening.
He died too soon to weep at its disgrace.

Graft is refined among the tea and scones,
Bluster (new style) invokes the public good,
And doing-down gets done in pious tones
Sam had tried to put on, but never could.

After Goliath

What shall be done to the man
that killeth this Philistine?
                    1 Sam. xvii, 26

The first shot out of that sling
Was enough to finish the thing:
The champion laid out cold
Before half the programmes were sold.
And then, what howls of dismay
From his fans in their dense array:
From aldermen, adjutants, aunts,
Administrators of grants,
Assurance-men, auctioneers,
Advisers about careers,
And advertisers, of course,
Plus the obvious b——s in force:
The whole reprehensible throng
Ten times an alphabet strong.
But such an auspicious debut
Was a little too good to be true,
Our victor sensed; the applause
From those who supported his cause
Sounded shrill and excessive now,
And who were they, anyhow?
Academics, actors who lecture,
Apostles of architecture,
Ancient-gods-of-the-abdomen men,
Angst-pushers, adherents of Zen,
Alastors, Austenites, A-test
Abolishers – even the straightest
Of issues looks pretty oblique

When a movement turns into a clique,
The conqueror mused, as he stopped
By the sword his opponent had dropped
Trophy, or means of attack
On the rapturous crowd at his back?
He shrugged and left it, resigned
To a new battle, fought in the mind,
For faith that his quarrel was just,
That the right man lay in the dust.

Sight Unseen

As I was waiting for the bus
  A girl came up the street,
Detectable as double-plus
  At seven hundred feet.

Her head was high, her step was free,
  Her face a lyric blur;
Her waist was narrow, I could see,
  But not the rest of her.

At fifty feet I watched her stop,
  Bite at a glove, then veer
Aside into some pointless shop,
  Never to reappear.

This happens every bloody day:
  They about-turn, they duck
Into their car and drive away,
  They hide behind a truck.

Look, if they knew me – understood,
  There might be cause to run;
Or if they saw me, well and good;
  And yet they don't, not one.

Love at first sight – by this we mean
  A stellar entrant thrown
Clear on the psyche's radar-screen,
  Recognized before known.

All right: things work the opposite
  Way with the poles reversed;
It's galling, though, when girls omit
  To switch the set on first.

Nothing to Fear

All fixed: early arrival at the flat
Lent by a friend, whose note says *Lucky sod*;
Drinks on the tray; the cover-story pat
And quite uncheckable; her husband off
Somewhere with all the kids till six o'clock
(Which ought to be quite long enough);
And all worth while: face really beautiful,
Good legs and hips, and as for breasts – my God.
What about guilt, compunction and such stuff?
I've had my fill of all that cock;
It'll wear off, as usual.

Yes, all fixed. Then why this slight trembling,
Dry mouth, quick pulse-rate, sweaty hands,
As though she were the first? No, not impatience,
Nor fear of failure, thank you, Jack.
Beauty, they tell me, is a dangerous thing,
Whose touch will burn, but I'm asbestos, see?
All worth while – it's a dead coincidence
That sitting here, a bag of glands
Tuned up to concert pitch, I seem to sense
A different style of caller at my back,
As cold as ice, but just as set on me.

Toys

A rattle, a woollen ball,
A cuddly animal
Are expendable.
A flameproof nightdress
(5–7 years)
Is pretty. Water-colours
And painting-book will
Keep someone out of trouble
And not make much mess.

Across the aisle are tiers
Of stuff we use on others
As soon as we can: men's
Two-tone cardigans;
Earrings; rings; pens.

Souvenirs

Photographs are dispensable.
The living, the still young,
Demand no such memorial.

Accusing letters still accuse,
Like the non-accusing.
No harm to be rid of those.

The mind will take surgery.
Though drink, resentment, self-
Defence impair the memory,

Something remains to be cut out.
God, car accident, stroke
Must do to remove it,

For the body adjoins the limb.
Who, heart back to normal,
Could himself cut off his own arm?

A Point of Logic

Love is a finding-out:
Our walk to the bedroom
(Hand in hand, eye to eye)
Up a stair of marble
Or decently scrubbed boards,
As much as what we do
In our abandonment,
Teaches us who we are
And what we are, and what
Life itself is.

Therefore put out the light,
Lurch to the bare attic
Over buckets of waste
And labouring bodies;
Leave the door wide open
And fall on each other,
Clothes barely wrenched aside;
Stay only a minute,
Depart separately,
And use no names.

On a Portrait of
Mme Rimsky-Korsakov

Serene, not as a prize for conflict won,
But mark of never having had to fight,
Needing no mind, because too beautiful,
She sat embodying her unconcern
For all charades of love or symbolism.
   Nicholas was inspecting a brass band,
   Driving to lunch with Borodin and Cui,
   Checking the full score of *The Snow Maiden*.

That dateless look, impersonal above
The coarse placing of the heart's Hollywood,
Writes off poor Janey Morris as a paddler
In joy and agony, a pop-eyed clown
Skinny and thick-lipped with her pomegranate.
   The Snow Maiden and the rest of the stuff
   Attain the permanence of print, wax, and
   Footnotes in treatises on orchestration.

A Chromatic Passing-Note

'That slimy tune' I said, and got a laugh,
In the middle of old Franck's D minor thing:
The dotted-rhythm clarinet motif.

Not always slimy. I thought, at fifteen,
It went to show that real love was found
At the far end of the right country lane.

I thought that, like Keats and the rest of them,
Old Franck was giving me a preview of
The world, action in art, a paradigm.

Yes, I know better now, or different.
Not image: buffer only, syrup, crutch.
'Slimy' was a snarl of disappointment.

Science Fiction

What makes us rove that starlit corridor
May be the impulse to meet face to face
Our vice and folly shaped into a thing,
And so at last ourselves; what lures us there
Is simpler versions of disaster :
A web that shuffles time and space,
A sentence to perpetual journeying,
A world of ocean without shore,
And simplest, flapping down the poisoned air,
A ten-clawed monster.

In him, perhaps, we see the general ogre
Who rode our ancestors to nightmare,
And in his habitat their maps of hell.
But climates and geographies soon change,
Spawning mutations none can quell
With silver sword or necromancer's ring,
Worse than their sires, of wider range,
And much more durable.

The Huge Artifice

an interim assessment

Enough of this great work has now appeared
For sightings to be taken, the ground cleared,
Though the main purpose – *what it's all about*
In the thematic sense – remains in doubt.
We can be certain, even at this stage,
That seriousness adequate to engage
Our deepest critical concern is not
To be found here. First : what there is of plot
Is thin, repetitive, leaning far too much
On casual meetings, parties, fights and such,
With that excessive use of coincidence
Which betrays authorial inexperience.
We note, besides these evident signs of haste,
A great deal in most questionable taste :
Too many sex-scenes, far too many coarse
Jokes, most of which have long lost all their force.

It might be felt that, after a slow start,
Abundant incident made amends for art,
But the work's 'greatness' is no more than size,
While the shaping mind, and all that that implies,
Is on a trivial scale, as can be guessed
From the brash nature of the views expressed
By a figure in an early episode, who
Was clearly introduced in order to
Act as some kind of author-surrogate,
Then hastily killed off – an unfortunate
Bid to retrieve a grave strategic lapse.

More damaging than any of this, the gaps
In sensitivity displayed are vast.

Concepts that have not often been surpassed
For ignorance or downright nastiness –
That the habit of indifference is less
Destructive than the embrace of love, that crimes
Are paid for never or a thousand times,
That the gentle come to grief – all these are forced
Into scenes, dialogue, comment, and endorsed
By the main action, manifesting there
An inhumanity beyond despair.

One final point remains : it has been urged
That a few characters are not quite submerged
In all this rubbish, that they can display
Reason, justice and forethought on their day,
And that this partly exculpates the mind
That was their author. Not at all. We find
Many of these in the history of art
(So this reviewer feels), who stand apart,
Who by no purpose but their own begin
To struggle free from a base origin.

New Approach Needed

Should you revisit us,
Stay a little longer,
And get to know the place.
Experience hunger,
Madness, disease and war.
You heard about them, true,
The last time you came here;
It's different having them.
And what about a go
At love, marriage, children?
All good, but bringing some
Risk of remorse and pain
And fear of an odd sort:
A sort one should, again,
Feel, not just hear about,
To be qualified as
A human-race expert.
On local life, we trust
The resident witness,
Not the royal tourist.

People have suffered worse
And more durable wrongs
Than you did on that cross
(I know – you won't get me
Up on one of those things),
Without sure prospect of
Ascending good as new
On the third day, without
'I die, but man shall live'
As a nice cheering thought.

So, next time, come off it,
And get some service in,
Jack, long before you start
Laying down the old law:
If you still want to then.
Tell your dad that from me.

Larger Truth

Round Fforestfach, Llansamlet and elsewhere
Some people, it being half past five,
Are going home from work, or whatever they do,
 Or wherever they live.

Others work at night, or are still working
At more different things than I could name,
Or work further away; wherever I stood
 I wouldn't see any of them.

It takes a novelist to say In Swansea
[Let's see the large-scale map] people [all right]
Were [as one man?] packing up work [one kind?]
 And going home [one street?].

Don't plead it's shorthand: he's not done yet.
He sardine-tins us but he plots too,
Merrily tabulating what we're up to,
 And what we think we're up to.

(That is our *donnée*, as it were, *mon bon*,
Our art's vast pattern-from-chaos complex –
Latent meaning exposed as it must be
 By a few swift strokes.)

It takes a poet to be more dishonest,
To pick stuff like this for his harangue,
To pretend that finding or withholding meaning
 Means anything.

Fiction

Today's last pensioner
Read to and washed up for,
The latest arrival
Weighed and pronounced bonny,
Nurse Lee, her broad shoulders
Trustworthiness itself,
Cycles into the dusk
Thinking of her teapot
And its comfort and cheer –
Adcock's No. 1 Brew
(Now only 2/8).

With this rubbed in, we go
Back to 'Gun Law' Part 3,
Where Eli Crumpacker,
A slug through his left arm,
Sways off in the saddle
To rouse the local slobs
Against Sheriff Billings,
And fix to have him shot
Right there in the court-house.
Eli's real poison, but
We know he won't get far.

They – this chap and Nurse Lee –
Are pretty nicely off:
She not scratching gnat-bites,
He with his rent paid up.
Lear just did what Lear did.
Fiction, where that is that

And will stay that, leaves me
Back here again, jealous
To see sorts of people
That feel their there and then,
That move from thing to thing.

L'Invitation au Voyage

—Welcome aboard the *Nautilus*, monsieur!
I vow you shall confess yourself amazed
Ten thousand times before our cruise is done.
What spectacles are mustered in the deep!
Beauty mere words are useless to depict,
Marvels unknown to science—dangers too,
Which we expunge with electricity.
Salute your comrades now: Ned Land, Conseil,
Brave fellows, and Professor Aronnax,
The eminent pelagiologist,
Whose fund of knowledge is at your desire,
As is my library, well-stocked and calm,
Matchless for the conducting of research.
Should you set store by music, you will find
That organ a trustworthy instrument,
While, for comestibles, we pride ourselves
On our sea-urchin loaf and shark ragout.
   Till dinner, then ...

—Thanks, Captain Nemo, this is always what
I think I want. But after weeks of Ned
On whaling, good Conseil just being good,
And Aronnax as Aronnax, I might
Start to browse round that matchless library,
Thrum at the organ, savour the thick film
Choking my tongue; and if, one afternoon,
A mermaid swam from the dead coral-groves
And looked in, sea-eyed, at the fat window,
Her olive hair writhing about her head,
Her turquoise nipples pried at by small fish,
Someone like me would say: 'Remarkable!

Behold, my friends, a rare phenomenon!
Doubtless, the lungs have been replaced by gills,
The hide, withstanding eighty atmospheres,
Moreover toughened – the Creator's hand
Lavish as always with new wonderment!'
   The long-boat, please...

Coming of Age

Twenty years ago he slipped into town,
A spiritual secret agent; took
Rooms right in the cathedral close; wrote down
Verbatim all their direst idioms;
Made phonetic transcripts in his black book;
Mimicked their dress, their gestures as they sat
Chaffering and chaffing in the Grand Hotel;
Infiltrated their glass-and-plastic homes,
Watched from the inside; then – his deadliest blow –
Went and married one of them (what about that?);
At the first christening played his part so well
That he started living it from then on,
His trick of camouflage no longer a trick.
Isn't it the spy's rarest triumph to grow
Indistinguishable from the spied upon,
The stick insect's to become a stick?

A.E.H.

Flame the westward skies adorning
Leaves no like on holt or hill;
Sounds of battle joined at morning
Wane and wander and are still.

Past the standards rent and muddied,
Past the careless heaps of slain,
Stalks a redcoat who, unbloodied,
Weeps with fury, not from pain.

Wounded lads, when to renew them
Death and surgeons cross the shade,
Still their cries, hug darkness to them;
All at last in sleep are laid.

All save one, who nightlong curses
Wounds imagined more than seen,
Who in level tones rehearses
What the fact of wounds must mean.

Oligodora

Open the casket
And accept these gifts,
All I can offer:
A small silver coin
Rubbed smooth by handling,
An unwrapped half-ounce
Of dust and gold-dust,
An emerald, flawed.

This is too little?
Am I in default,
Or are you grasping?
Which of us shows more
Inadequacy?

Green Heart

Cromyomancy* carves out a preview
And a foretaste of you:
Brittle as gold-leaf the outer skin,
Firmness within;
Full savour, more piercing than any
Peach or strawberry;
The heart will grow.

From the beginning, tears flow,
But of no rage or grief:
Wise cromyomancers know
Weeping augurs belief.

* Divination by means of onions.

Waking Beauty

Finding you was easy.
At each machete-stroke
The briers—neatly tagged
By Freud the gardener—
Fell apart like cut yarn.
Your door was unfastened.
You awoke instantly,
Returning that first kiss
As in no mere fable.

But how should I return
Through far thornier tracts
Of the wild rose-jungle,
Dry, aching, encumbered
By a still-drowsy girl?

Your eyes cleared and steadied.
Side by side we advanced
On those glossy giants
And their lattice of barbs:
But they had all withered.

An Attempt at Time-Travel

Your father had the reins.
He chatted over his shoulder,
Laughing, showing white teeth
Between brown moustache and beard.
His brown bowler was festive.

Next to me, your grandfather,
In a grey suit, clean-shaven,
Smiled a little, watching
The tall horse move. At his fob
A lovely big watch swung.

But you, nine years old
In azure satin blue-trimmed,
Neither turned nor spoke.
At ten, this defeated me.
But at thirty? Twenty?

In Memoriam W.R.A.

ob. April 18th, 1963

A *Cricket Match*, between
  The *Gentlemen of Cambridge*
And the *Hanover Club*, to be played
By the *Antient Laws* of the *Game*
[Two stumps, no boundaries, lobs,
Single wicket, no pads – all that]
  In *Antient Costume*
  For a *Good Cause*.

Leading the Gentlemen,
  I won the toss and batted.
With a bat like an overgrown spoon
And a racquets ball, runs came fast;
But as, in my ruffles and tights,
I marched to the crease, I was sad
  To see you nowhere
  About the field.

You would have got the point:
  'No boundaries' meant running
Literally each bloody run.
When I 'threw my wicket away'
And, puffing, limped back to my seat,
I wanted to catch your eye
  Half-shut with laughter
  (And pride and love).

Afterwards, over pints,
  Part of a chatting circle,
You would have said I was right
To declare about when I did;

Though the other chaps went for the runs
And got them with plenty in hand,
   What does it matter?
   The game's the thing.

   Later: the two of us:
   'That time – do you remember? –
We watched Wally Hammond at Lord's,
And you said you wished you were him,
And I fixed up a coach, but you said
You were working too hard for exams?
   Oh well. A pity
   You never tried.'

   I know. And I foresee
   (As if this were not fancy)
The on-and-on of your talk,
My gradually formal response
That I could never defend
But never would soften enough,
   Leading to silence,
   And separate ways.

   Forgive me if I have
   To see it as it happened:
Even your pride and your love
Have taken this time to become
Clear, to arouse my love.
I'm sorry you had to die
   To make me sorry
   You're not here now.

The Evans Country

Dedicated to the Patrons and Staff
of the Newton Inn, Mumbles, Swansea

There's more to local life today
I know, than what I've found to say;
But when you start recording it
You've got to tone it down a bit.

Aberdarcy: the Main Square

By the new Boots, a tool-chest with flagpoles
Glued on, and flanges, and a dirty great
Baronial doorway, and things like port-holes,
Evans met Mrs Rhys on their first date.

Beau Nash House, that sells Clothes for Gentlemen,
Jacobethan, every beam nailed on tight –
Real wood, though, mind you – was in full view when,
Lunching at the Three Lamps, she said all right.

And he dropped her beside the grimy hunk
Of castle, that with luck might one day fall
On to the *Evening Post*, the time they slunk
Back from that lousy week-end in Porthcawl.

The journal of some bunch of architects
Named this the worst town centre they could find;
But how disparage what so well reflects
Permanent tendencies of heart and mind?

All love demands a witness: something 'there'
Which it yet makes part of itself. These two
Might find Carlton House Terrace, St Mark's Square,
A bit on the grand side. What about you?

St Asaph's

A chestnut tree stands in the line of sight
Between the GIRLS entrance and 'Braich-y-Pwll',
Where, half past eightish, Evans shaves his face,
    Squints out the window.

Not that he really wants to get among
Schoolchildren – see, some of the stuff by there,
All bounce and flounce, rates keeping an eye on:
    Forthcoming models.

It's tough, though. Past the winter boughs he'll spot
Bunches of overcoats quite clear; come May,
Just the odd flash of well-filled gingham, and
    Stacks of rich verdure.

You can't win, Dai. Nature's got all the cards.
But bear up: you still know the bloody leaf
From bole or blossom, dancer from the dance.
    Hope for you yet, then.

Langwell

'Now then, what are you up to, Dai?'
'Having a little bonfire, pet.'
   Bowed down under a sack,
With steps deliberate and sly,
His deacon's face full of regret,
   Evans went out the back.

Where no bugger could overlook
He dumped into a blackened bin
   Sheaves of photogravure,
Now and then an ill-printed book,
Letters in female hands: the thin
   Detritus of amour.

Paraffin-heightened flames made ash
Of *Lorraine Burnet in 3-D*
   And *I'm counting the days*
And *the head girl took off her sash*
And *Naturist* and *can we be*
   Together for always?

He piped an eye – only the smoke –
Then left that cooling hecatomb
   And dashed up to his den,
Where the real hot stuff was. A bloke
Can't give any old tripe house-room:
   Style's something else again.

Pendydd

Love is like butter, Evans mused, and stuck
The last pat on his toast. Breakfast in bed
At the Red Dragon – when Miss Protheroe,
Wearing her weekday suit, had caught the train
Back home, or rather to her place of work,
United Mutual Trust – encouraged thought,
And so did the try-asking-me-then look
The bird who fetched the food had given him.
Scrub that for now. Love is like butter. It
Costs money but, fair play, not all that much,
However hard you go at it there's more,
Though to have nothing else would turn you up
(Like those two fellows on that raft*, was it?),
Nothing spreads thinner when you're running short;
Natural? Well, yes and no. Better than guns,
And – never mind what the heart experts say –
Let's face it, bloody good for you. Dead odd
That two things should turn out so much alike,
He thought, ringing the bell for more of both.

* Dinghy, actually. Evans is thinking of an episode in *The
Bombard Story* (Penguin edition, p. 17).

Llansili Beach

In his new bather – pretty grand,
Quite frankly – lounging on the sand,
Evans relaxes with the warm
Sun on his back, and studies form.
He lights a fag. Inside a minute
A two-piece with a fair lot in it
Rolls up between him and the sea.
Now watch, and listen, carefully.
He dives straight for his coat, pulls out
His glasses, shoves them on his snout;
Demeanour, casual; gaze, intent.
Years back, he'd have done different:
Whipped off the buggers – anyhow,
Not calmly stuck them on. But now
He stands four-eyed and unashamed,
Also, and here's the point, untamed.
No heartfelt gaze'll satisfy
A real romantic like our Dai;
Wouldn't be natural for a bloke.
He's off: 'Hallo. Care for a smoke?'
Your look/do ratio doesn't change.
All that might is your visual range.

Brynbwrla

Love's domain, supernal Zion,
  How thy rampart gleams with light,
Beacon to the wayworn pilgrim
  Stoutly faring through the night!

Some, their eyes on heavenly mansions,
  Tread the road their fathers trod,
Others, whom the Foe hath blinded,
  Far asunder stray from God.

And still others – take old Evans –
  Anchor on their jack instead;
Zion, pro- or non- or anti-,
  Never got them out of bed.

Light's abode? There stands the chapel,
  Flat and black against the sky.
Tall hotels ablaze with neon
  Magnetise the sons of Dai.

Maunders

In the Casino Ballroom,
   The judges disagree
– Some leading local ladies:
   Dai Evans: a J.P. –
On picking Miss Glamorgan
   (West) 1963.

'No, Mr Wynne – on poise, now,
   Miss Clydach just won't do;
And as for, well, her figure,
   It's too … too much on view.
Your vote, please, Mr Evans,'
   Smiles Mrs Town Clerk Pugh.

Dai's seen in Clydach's hip-swing,
   Rich bosom and mean face,
Two threats: his own destruction
   By passion's fell embrace,
Or else (a bit more likely)
   Not getting to first base;

Whereas Pugh's time of danger
   Belongs to yesterday,
When choice was more than hedging,
   Reluctance than delay.
– Dai votes against Miss Clydach,
   Then waits his chance to say:

'This show's for youngsters, really.
   The dance'll soon begin,
So why don't you and I, love,
   Pop up the Newlands Inn,
And strengthen our acquaintance
   Over a spot of gin?'

Fforestfawr

When they saw off Dai Evans's da
The whole thing was done very nice:
Bethesda was packed to the doors,
And the minister, Urien Price,
Addressed them with telling effect.

'Our brother grew rich in respect,'
He told them in accents of fire;
'A man of unshakable strength,
Whom to know was at once to admire.
He did nothing common or mean.'

They'd no notion of coming between
That poor young Dai and his grief,
So each of them just had a word
With him after, well-chosen and brief:
'I looked up to him, boy' sort of touch.

He thanked one and all very much,
But thought, as he waved them goodbye,
Was respect going to be what they felt
When Bethesda did honour to Dai?
No, something more personal, see?

'Hallo, pet. Alone? Good. It's me.
Ah now, who did you think it was?
Well, come down the Bush and find out.
You'll know me easy, because
I'm wearing a black tie, love.'

Welch Ferry, West Side

The narrow channel where the tankers crawl
And void their cargo into the pipelines,
Encloses, with the railway track that runs
Down to the tinplate works, a chunk of hill,
And here sometimes a pony browses.

Above, on the side farthest from the town,
Beneath the ridge long shorn of pit-prop timber,
A shooting-brake, a 1960 Humber,
Sometimes pulls in among the gorse, unseen :
Evans is careful with his courting.

Last night, leaving Miss Jones to powder her
Nose in the back, he got out for a stroll,
And noticed – right enough his head was full
Of *oh, you know I do* and *are you sure?*
And *darling, please* and *you're the sweetest* –

That all the smog had lifted, and more stars
Than he knew what to do with filled the sky,
And lighted lighthouse, civic centre, quay,
Chimneys, the pony's pasture, cooling-towers;
'Looks beautiful tonight,' he muttered,

Then raised his voice : 'Eurwen, get moving, do.
You think I want to hang round here all night?
Free over the week-end, are you? I'm not;
I'm boozing with the boys on Saturday,
Sunday's the club ... All right, then – never.'

Aldport (Mystery Tour)

Hearing how tourists, dazed with reverence,
Look through sunglasses at the Parthenon,
Dai thought of that cold night outside the Gents
When he touched Dilys up with his gloves on.

Aberdarcy: the Chaucer Road

5.40. The Bay View. After the office,
Evans drops in for a quick glass of stout,
Then, by the fruit-machine, runs into Haydn,
Who's marrying the kid he's nuts about.

Of course, he won't pretend it's all been easy:
The wife's three-quarters off her bloody head,
And Gwyneth being younger than their youngest
Leaves certain snags still to be combated.

Oh, no gainsaying that she's quite a handful;
No, not bad-tempered, man, just a bit wild.
He likes a girl to show a touch of spirit;
It's all the better when you're reconciled.

And then, dear dear, what dizzy peaks of passion!
Not only sex, but mind and spirit too,
Like in that thing Prof Hughes took with the Honours:
That's right, *The Rainbow* – well, it's all come true.

6.10. The Humber. Evans starts reflecting
How much in life he's never going to know:
All it must mean to really love a woman.
He pulls up sharp outside a bungalow.

6.30. Balls to where. In like a whippet;
A fearsome thrash with Mrs No-holds-barred
(Whose husband's in his surgery till 7);
Back at the wheel 6.50, breathing hard.

7.10. 'Braich-y-Pwll'. – 'Hallo now, Megan.
No worse than usual, love. You been all right?
Well, this looks good. And there's a lot on later;
Don't think I'll bother with the club tonight.'

Nice bit of haddock with poached egg, Dundee cake,
Buckets of tea, then a light ale or two,
And 'Gun Smoke', 'Danger Man', the Late Night Movie –
Who's doing better, then? What about you?